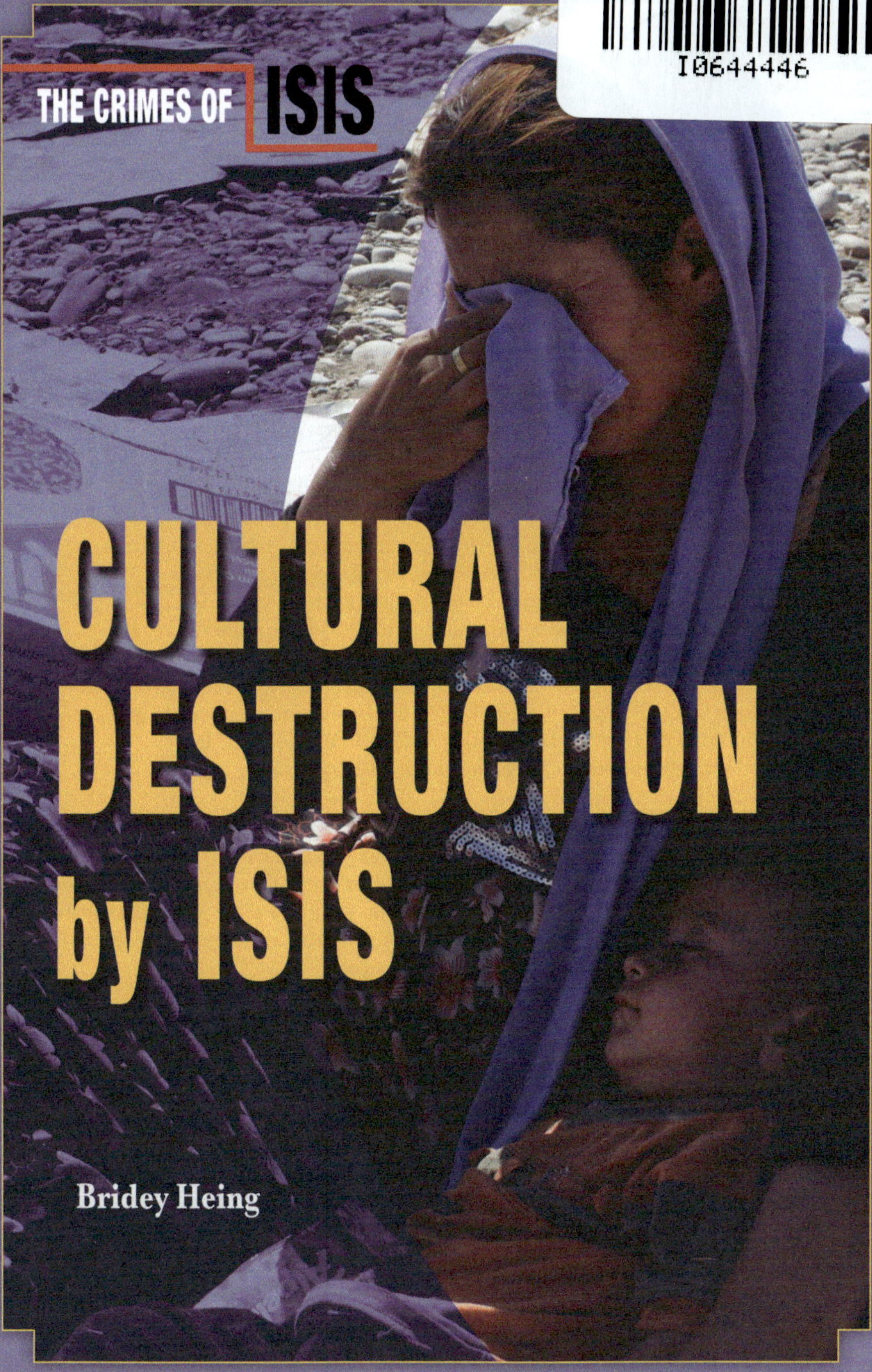

THE CRIMES OF ISIS

CULTURAL DESTRUCTION by ISIS

Bridey Heing

Enslow Publishing
101 W. 23rd Street
Suite 240
New York, NY 10011
USA
enslow.com

Published in 2018 by Enslow Publishing, LLC.
101 W. 23rd Street, Suite 240, New York, NY 10011

Library of Congress Cataloging-in-Publication Data

Names: Heing, Bridey, author.
Title: Cultural destruction by ISIS / by Bridey Heing.
Description: New York : Enslow Publishing, 2018. | Series: The crimes of ISIS | Includes bibliographical references and index. | Audience: Grades 7–12.
Identifiers: LCCN 2017026280 | ISBN 9780766092150 (library bound) | ISBN 9780766095830 (paperback)
Subjects: LCSH: Iraq—Antiquities—Juvenile literature. | Syria—Antiquities—Juvenile literature. | Iraq—Civilization—Juvenile literature. | Syria—Civilization—Juvenile literature. | Cultural property—Destruction and pillage—Iraq—History—21st century—Juvenile literature. | Cultural property—Destruction and pillage—Syria—History—21st century—Juvenile literature. | Cultural property—Protection—Iraq—Juvenile literature. | Cultural property—Protection—Syria—Juvenile literature. | IS (Organization)—Juvenile literature.
Classification: LCC DS69.6 .H435 2018 | DDC 364.16/4—dc23
LC record available at https://lccn.loc.gov/2017026280

Printed in the United States of America

To Our Readers: We have done our best to make sure all website addresses in this book were active and appropriate when we went to press. However, the author and the publisher have no control over and assume no liability for the material available on those websites or on any websites they may link to. Any comments or suggestions can be sent by email to customerservice@enslow.com.

Photo Credits: Cover, p. 1 Sebastian Meyer/Corbis/Getty Images; p. 4 Yunus Keles/Anadolu Agency/Getty Images; pp. 6–7 © AP Images; p. 10 Ali Muhammed/Anadolu Agency/Getty Images; pp. 12–13 Mohamad Abazeed/AFP/Getty Images; pp. 14–15 Culture Club/Hulton Archive/Getty Images; pp. 18–19, 34–35, 52–53 Ahmad Al-Rubaye/AFP/Getty Images; pp. 24–25 Martyn Aim/Getty Images; pp. 26–27 Fethi Belaid/AFP/Getty Images; pp. 30–31 Ahmad Gharabli/AFP/Getty Images; pp. 36–37 Carl Court/Getty Images; pp. 40–41 Fadel Senna/AFP/Getty Images; pp. 42–43 Safin Hamed/AFP/Getty Images; pp. 46–47 Aris Messinis/AFP/Getty Images; pp. 50–51, 78–79, 82 Sabah Arar/AFP/Getty Images; pp. 56–57 Russian Defence Ministry Press Office/TASS/Getty Images; pp. 58–59, 62–63, 92–93 Louai Beshara/AFP/Getty Images; p. 64 Michael Nicholson/Corbis/Getty Images; p. 67 DEA/DeAgostini/Getty Images; pp. 72–73 Dimitar Dilkoff/AFP/Getty Images; pp. 74–75 Uygar Onder Simsek/AFP/Getty Images; p. 84 Charles Platiau/AFP/Getty Images; p. 86 Richard Baker/In Pictures/Getty Images; pp. 88–89 Alberto PizzoliAFP/Getty Images.

CONTENTS

Iraqi soldiers inspect the Mosul Museum in 2017. The museum is just one of many cultural sites across Iraq and Syria that ISIS has targeted in its attempt to erase all aspects of history and religion with which it disagrees.

INTRODUCTION:

ERASING HISTORY

The Middle East has been one of the most important centers of human civilization for thousands of years, and today it is home to numerous ruins and archaeological sites that provide insight into life in the ancient world. But these sites are under threat due to the rise of the Islamic State of Iraq and Syria, or ISIS. The group that swept to power in 2014 and has since horrified the world with their brutality has continuously looted and destroyed heritage sites in their territory in an attempt to turn back the hands of time to match their perception of what a true Islamic society looks like.

ISIS is a fundamentalist Salafist group led by Abu Bakr al-Baghdadi, a largely secretive leader who espouses an ideology rooted in hate and violence. He and his followers want to establish a caliphate, or religiously run Islamic state, which he declared shortly after taking control of Mosul in Iraq in 2014. The caliphate ISIS desires would return the Islamic world to the kind of life Muslims had shortly after the death of the prophet Muhammad in the 700s CE. In order to achieve their goal, the group has worked to completely eradicate all non-Islamic influence, including religions that are not in line with their strict and literal interpretation of Sunni teachings and destroying structures that are defined as pre-Islamic. These structures include palaces, tombs, temples, and cities that have stood for thousands of years in Syria and Iraq.

From Palmyra in Syria to Nineveh in Iraq, ISIS has used cultural destruction as a means to rewrite history in hopes of forcing citizens in their territory to identify more heavily with the group than with their national identities. Leaning on religious teachings that highlight norms of war from centuries ago, the group thinks of destruction as a way to exert control and spread an image of themselves as powerful and impossible to hold accountable. They also loot artifacts to sell on the black market, a trade that has generated an untold amount of money and has become one of their primary income streams.

It is true that ISIS is not the first group to use destruction to show their power. In ancient times, destruction was a way to force populations to convert or fall in line. In more modern times, it is a practice that is internationally taboo and thus a draw for

Muslim pilgrims visit the famous al-Askari mosque in Samarra, Iraq, in 2004. In 2006, al-Qaeda bombed the mosque, destroying its famous gold dome.

extremist organizations looking to make a statement. Al-Qaeda and other terrorist organizations have destroyed antiquities to show their influence and ability to reshape the world. Today, ISIS hopes to tap into the same authority.

But the international community is working against them. Organizations like UNESCO, the governing body of the United Nations that handles World Heritage Sites and cultural products, has been proactive in their work to safeguard and defend these spaces, while other groups are working to raise awareness of their importance. Others still are working to document the damage ISIS is doing in hopes of one day holding the group accountable for their violations of international law. Although the fight is far from over and some antiquities will never be salvaged, the ground is being laid now to ensure that ISIS does not get away with what amounts to cultural erasure.

1

THE HEART OF THE ANCIENT WORLD

Today, ISIS is primarily active in the Middle East, in a swath of territory that crosses the Syria-Iraq border. Areas under their control include cities and ruins that date back to antiquity and span empires, religions, and cultures. The Middle East has long been a diverse part of the world, thanks in large part to its importance in international trade and its place along important trade routes, like the Silk Road. That blending of cultures made the region one of the most vital in the world, a center of learning, artistic expression, literature, and architecture where some of the most important discoveries in numerous fields were made. Today, monuments to the region's importance to human history stand across the Middle East, including shrines, the ruins of grand buildings, and cultural artifacts in museums.

ISIS has made it a primary goal to erase that history by physically destroying items they feel do not represent the so-called pure Islam they hope to reinstate. Before we learn about how cultural destruction fits into their ideology and

Iraqi Defense Minister Khaled al-Obeidi (*left*) and Lieutenant General Abdul Amir al-Shammari (*right*) study a map of Iraq while planning a fight to free the city of Fallujah from ISIS control in May 2016.

strategy, it is important to understand what the artifacts and ruins they are targeting mean for global and regional heritage.

For most of history, the area we know as the Middle East was not divided into states. The British and French drew the modern borders following the collapse of the Ottoman Empire in the 1920s. Before that, the region was controlled and governed by a series of empires and kingdoms, including the Romans, Persians, Babylonians, Mongols, and others. At times, multiple empires or kingdoms ruled in the region, while at others the area was controlled primarily by one or two central forces. In this chapter, Syria and Iraq are used to refer to the territory that falls under the modern states, but often the governing body that ruled over one also controlled the other.

A CENTER FOR TRADE

The Middle East has long been a center of global culture and thinking, thanks in no small part to its crucial role in global trade. Trade is a means by which cultures spread and grow, giving rise to alliances, exchanges, and mutual development around the world. In antiquity, trade flourished around the Middle East, including along the Silk Road in the east, the Mediterranean in the west, and India to the southwest. Numerous routes crisscrossed the land, and sea routes connected the Arab Peninsula to the rest of the world. Goods made in the Middle East, including dye developed by the Phoenicians and spices harvested in the region, became highly prized around the ancient world, driving wealth and status in the civilizations that thrived there. Trade brought merchants, scholars, and explorers from around the world to the Middle East, where they shared ideas and goods with others. The civilizations and empires of the region were truly the heart of the ancient world, connecting the East and West while allowing diversity to thrive under the rulers who grew wealthy off the flow of activity and currency. The cities reflect this diversity of religion, culture, design, and thought, highlighting the important role of the Middle East in shaping our modern world.

THE CRADLE OF CIVILIZATION

Modern Syria and Iraq have been home to people for tens of thousands of years, including some of mankind's earliest civilizations. Remains and artifacts dating from around 80,000 BCE, including Neanderthals, have been found in the area, and Mesopotamia was centered around Iraq and Syria starting in

A stone engraved with Islamic text is at the ancient Roman amphitheater of Bosra al-Sham in Syria. The location is one of many UNESCO sites in Iraq and Syria that are at risk of destruction.

approximately 10,000 BCE. Cities like Damascus and Baghdad were already established by around 3000 BCE, and they were considered centers of learning and study.

Throughout ancient history, different empires dominated the region, including the Assyrian Empire, the Egyptians, and the Persians. Syria fell to Rome in around 64 BCE, and Mesopotamia became part of the Roman Empire in the second century CE. When the area was under Roman rule, Syria was of particular importance, with the city of Antioch becoming the third largest in Roman territory and serving as an important trade hub. Cultures melded in cities like Palmyra, where ruins showed influence from both East and West. The region was also extremely diverse, with merchants and workers from around the world mingling and living together.

This part of the world was long a center of learning, up to and through the rise of Islam. Early forms of writing emerged in Mesopotamia, and Mesopotamia also developed the sixty-minute hour and the twenty-four–hour day, among other important mathematical innovations. Medicine and astronomy also developed under the Mesopotamians, and the arts of the region became globally recognized and coveted. That tradition of learning and exploration was strengthened with the rise of Islam, which swept the region in the seventh century.

THE ISLAMIC EMPIRE

Islam was established in the early seventh century by Muhammad, a prophet who went on to found the Islamic Empire. Because of Muhammad's early political power, which he was able to acquire after settling in what would become Medina, Saudi Arabia, where he served as a mediator of sorts between fighting tribes and groups, Islam evolved as both a political force and a religious doctrine. Through both military conquest and alliances, Muhammad was able to spread Islam and his own authority throughout the Arabian peninsula, and his political philosophy is reflected in Islamic teachings on taxes, governance, and other explicit policies.

After Muhammad's death in 632 CE, the Islamic Empire was ruled over by a series of four caliphs, known as the Rashidun (or rightly guided) Caliphate. These leaders were able to expand their empire south across North Africa, north to modern Turkey, and across modern Iran, and later caliphs conquered parts of Spain and north into Europe. Although there was infighting among Muslims following the schism between the Shia and Sunni factions, the Islamic Empire was largely one where education and innovation were at the heart of the leadership's interests.

The latter half of the eighth century is often considered one of the most prolific, under the Abbasid Caliphate. Literature, poetry, the arts, and science all made immense advances under the Abbasids, and formal centers of learning and religious development were founded under their reign. Universities were opened in the centuries to come, libraries became the envy of countries across the globe, and works were translated from languages around the world. Trade played a large role in bringing multiple cultures together in Islamic territory, influencing writing, philosophy, and architecture. Wealth was poured into building elaborate and beautiful buildings alongside the ancient ones that are now under threat.

The Islamic Empire eventually became the Ottoman Empire, which collapsed in the late 1910s following World War I. The Middle East, including Iraq and Syria, became part

A rare depiction of the prophet Muhammad was drawn circa 1314. Because Islam forbids pictures of the Prophet, ISIS seeks to destroy artifacts like this and erase them from memory.

RUMI

For much of history, literature and poetry have been some of the greatest cultural exports of the Middle East. Few figures from early Islamic culture stand taller than Rumi, a Sufi mystic poet who remains one of the best-selling poets in the world even today, with millions of copies of his translated works selling in the United States. Born in modern-day Afghanistan to a cleric father, he traveled extensively as a young boy and spent time in multiple centers of learning, including Baghdad and Damascus, where he spent time as an adult. Eventually, he and his family settled in Konya in the Persianate Sultanate of Rum, located in modern-day Turkey. There, Rumi gathered a significant following, thanks in part to his enthusiastic and often ecstatic poems that linked love, religion, nature, and compassion. His work illustrates the diversity of the region during his life, from around 1207 CE to 1273 CE. He wrote in Persian, Turkish, Arabic, and Greek, and he embraced practices that ranged from Sufi mysticism to Dervish dancing to Sunni traditions. He lived in a diverse city, where he won the loyalty of Jews, Christians, and other practitioners of various faiths. When he died, a great funeral was held, and today a shrine sits at his tomb in Konya, which draws pilgrims from around the world who wish to pay homage to the great poet and theologian.

of a British and French mandate. The two countries carved the region into states with the Sykes-Picot Agreement, and Syria was put under French control, while Iraq was governed by the British. The detrimental role of colonization in shaping the culture and politics of these places quickly gave rise to groups that embraced earlier philosophy about the rejection of Western influence in favor of a purely Islamic religious and ethnic identity; some of them have gone on to become legitimate political parties, while others remain terrorist or fringe organizations.

ISIS has declared itself a caliphate, referring to the early days of Islam when all Muslims recognized the religious and political authority of the caliph, or leader. The group claims to want to return to a society that reflects the values and ways of earlier Islamic leaders, including the Rashidun Caliphate. But their view of that time ignores the fact that Islam has always been synonymous with learning and innovation, pushing mankind forward even during the European Dark Ages. Rather than being rooted in the reality of what Islam has meant in history, groups like ISIS are reactionary against the spread and influence of Western culture, rejection of Western hegemony, and unbridled hatred that they try to rationalize by pulling selectively from religious texts and teachings. They also overlook the fact that Muslims around the world have rejected the religious and political authority al-Baghdadi and his followers have sought to claim, undermining his power.

CULTURAL HERITAGE & INTERNATIONAL LAW

The level of cultural destruction that ISIS has committed is deplorable and has drawn condemnation from around the world. But is it illegal? International law is complex and often difficult to enforce, particularly during war, when access to evidence of crime and those responsible is heavily limited. But

The ancient city of Hatra, Iraq, is one of many UNESCO historical sites in the Middle East that ISIS has attacked. The city was built in the third or second century BCE, and it survived thousands of years before ISIS occupied the area in 2014.

there are statutes and precedents that are intended to govern the protection of heritage sites and artifacts.

One of the earliest laws governing the treatment of cultural heritage sites was the 1907 Hague IV Convention, which was one of the first to outline the responsibilities of states during wartime. Two articles in the convention apply to cultural heritage sites, artworks, and other noncombatant spaces.

Article 27 forbids the bombardment and other forms of assault on places like museums, hospitals, and other noncombatant spaces of cultural or charitable value. Article 56, which more explicitly applies to the kinds of destruction ISIS is engaged in, reads:

> The property of municipalities, that of institutions dedicated to religion, charity and education, the arts and sciences, even when State property, shall be treated as private property. All seizure of, destruction or wilful damage done to institutions of this character, historic monuments, works of art and science, is forbidden, and should be made the subject of legal proceedings.[1]

In 1970, the Convention on the Means of Prohibiting and Preventing the Illicit Import, Export and Transfer of Ownership of Cultural Property was passed by the United Nations to stop looting and sales of goods stolen from cultural sites. In 1972, the United Nations passed the Convention Concerning the Protection of the World Cultural and Natural Heritage, a treaty that binds member states to certain duties to protect cultural sites. The treaty requires that all signatory states put programs into place to conserve their heritage sites, which are recognized by the treaty as part of a global heritage and therefore a global responsibility.

But implementing these regulations is difficult, particularly against non-state actors that, by their nature, are not signatories on such treaties. To date, only one person has ever been charged with war crimes related to destruction of cultural sites; in 2016, Ahmed al-Faqi al-Mahdi was found guilty of taking part in the destruction of ancient sites in Timbuktu with al-Qaeda. He was charged under the International Criminal Court Rome Statute of 2002, in which Article 8 lists "extensive destruction and appropriation of property, not justified by military necessity and carried out unlawfully and wantonly" and "intentionally directing attacks against buildings dedicated to religion, education, art, science or charitable purposes, historic monuments, hospitals and places where the sick and wounded are collected, provided they are not military objectives" as war crimes.[2]

But prosecuting ISIS officials poses distinct problems. International warrants issued by the International Criminal Court (ICC) often can't be acted upon due to the lack of a central police force that can carry them out; instead, the warrant can be enacted by member states when the person against whom the warrant was issued enters their territory. In most cases, officials avoid this by staying in their own country or getting assurances they will not be arrested if they do visit another country. In the case of militants, by their nature they are difficult to arrest, often living in volatile areas where combat is common. Members of ISIS can hide in war-torn Syria, even if pushed out of Iraq, which means that even after the lengthy process of gathering evidence and making a case against them has been completed, they would be unlikely to face a trial.

Nonetheless, many have been vocal in their support for holding ISIS accountable for all their crimes, including those against cultural heritage sites. The United Nations Security Council issued a resolution in February 2015 stating that "all Member States shall take appropriate steps to prevent the trade in Iraqi and Syrian cultural property and other items of archaeological, historical, cultural, rare scientific, and religious importance illegally removed from Iraq since 6 August 1990 and from Syria since 15 March 2011," encompassing a period of time that includes looting by both ISIS and other terror groups that were active in the region. In May of that year, the General Assembly affirmed the body's concerns about the destruction of cultural heritage in Iraq, reading in part:

> Appalled by the destruction and looting carried out by the Islamic State in Iraq and the Levant (ISIL), also known as Daesh, of the cultural heritage of Iraq, cradle of the Mesopotamian civilization, found in its museums, libraries, archives and archaeological sites, places of worship, including mosques, shrines and churches, and of religious and cultural artefacts, which are irreparable losses for Iraq and for humanity as a whole; alarmed by the increasing number of intentional attacks against and threats to the cultural heritage of countries affected by armed conflict as well as the organized looting of and trafficking in cultural objects, which occurs on an unprecedented scale today; deeply concerned about such acts generating income for terrorist groups, which can support their recruitment efforts and strengthen their operational capability to organize and carry out terrorist attacks...Affirms that attacks intentionally directed against buildings dedicated to religion, education, art, science or charitable purposes, or historic monuments, may amount to war crimes...[3]

UNESCO has started a Global Coalition to Counter ISIS, a campaign called #United4Heritage, which rallies young people in Iraq to help them connect with their cultural heritage, and spearheads efforts to safeguard sites when territory is retaken by ISIS. The group has also been outspoken in their condemnation of ISIS's actions, summing up the global sense of horror at the ancient sites ISIS has destroyed.

"We cannot remain silent," UNESCO Director General Irina Bokova said in 2015 following the destruction of Nimrud, an ancient Iraqi city. "The deliberate destruction of cultural heritage constitutes a war crime. I call on all political and religious leaders in the region to stand up and remind everyone that there is absolutely no political or religious justification for the destruction of humanity's cultural heritage."[4]

2

AN IDEOLOGY OF DESTRUCTION

ISIS evolved into the group we know today over the span of nearly a decade, but from the very beginning its ideology was rooted in a belief in destruction and violence. It started as al-Qaeda in Iraq, a localized branch of al-Qaeda that swore allegiance to the group under Abu Musab al-Zarqawi in the early 2000s. But the two groups were at odds early on due to al-Zarqawi's practice of labeling other Muslims *takfiri*, or apostates. Doing so carried a death penalty for whoever he accused, and he didn't hesitate to act as judge and executioner himself. Although al-Qaeda was willing to target civilians, they did not encourage the targeted killing of Muslims or the brutal tactics al-Zarqawi was willing to employ.

It wasn't until 2010, after al-Zarqawi and a series of leaders who followed him were killed in airstrikes and operations, that the group we now know as ISIS began to develop. The group was not particularly influential early on, but was able to ride a wave of Sunni disenfranchisement in Iraq to swell their numbers and gain local support in 2009. Abu Bakr al-Baghdadi, a secretive

An Iraqi Emergency Response Division soldier stands in front of an ISIS mural at an underground ISIS training facility the ERD had raided. The mural reads "We will liberate Rome" in Arabic script.

man who was briefly held by US led forces, became the leader of what was then called the Islamic State in Iraq in 2010. When the Syrian Civil War broke out the following year, al-Baghdadi helped set up al-Nusra Front, a branch of al-Qaeda that still operates in Syria, but was discouraged from moving operations there from northern Iraq. But in early 2013, al-Baghdadi announced that he was combining al-Nusra Front and his own group to create the Islamic State of Iraq and the Levant (or Syria), although al-Nusra Front's leadership rebuffed his attempt to coopt them. Instead, he split with al-Qaeda and by early 2014 had begun claiming territory in Iraq and Syria, including Raqqa where the group is now headquartered.

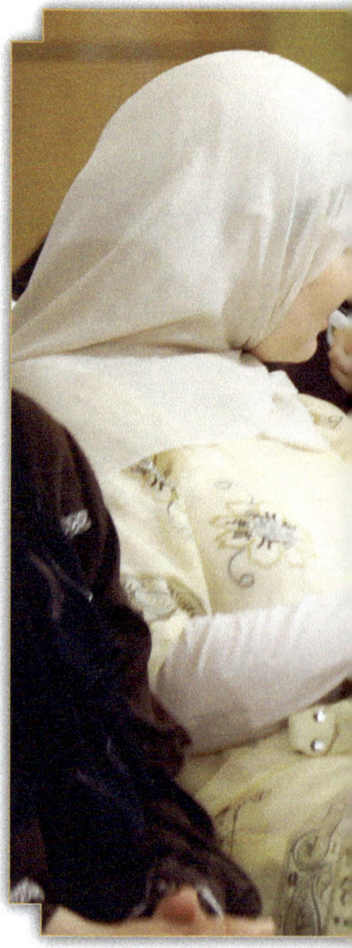

Since then, the group has become known as one of the most destructive and violent in recent history. They have engaged in targeted campaigns of ethnic cleansing, and they use extreme public punishments to control the populations living under their rule. For much of the world, their brutality seems random—and it is difficult to understand how a group that is so violent can possibly have an overarching and cohesive ideology. But for ISIS, destruction and violence are part of a complex strategy that reflects their values, beliefs, and goals.

SALAFISM & WAHHABISM

The ideology that drives ISIS can be traced to extremist strains of Salafism and Wahhabism, two separate schools of Islamic thought that are often used synonymously. ISIS themselves draw from both, sharing quotes from Wahhabist thinkers while embracing practices that are more in line with Salafism. Both schools of thought are rooted in a belief in the need to return to a "pure Islam," something ISIS has made a primary goal in their territory.

Veiled women attend the first congress of Tunisia's new ultra-conservative Salafist party. The group says that Salafism, which is the basis of ISIS's beliefs, can be compatible with democracy.

Wahhabism was established in the eighteenth century by Muhammad ibn 'Abd al-Wahhab, a scholar who advocated a return to the principles that guided the early followers of Islam. He advocated for an extreme rejection of Western influence and innovation, as well as religious icons that were not in keeping with Islamic teachings. He also advocated for the practice of Sharia law, or Islamic codes that dictate punishment for various crimes. These reforms were meant to "purify" Islam, in part through the killing of apostates and destruction of structures seen as linked to polytheist pre-Islamic faiths. Wahhabism was in part a rejection of colonialism, and it emerged alongside other schools of thought that advocated for a stronger sense of Muslim and Arab identity in the face of Western oppression. Wahhabism, however, became a political force when the House of Saud, which would become the ruling family of Saudi Arabia, aligned with the movement. That alliance has remained strong through today, and Wahhabism is widely associated with Saudi Arabia.

Salafism shares Wahhabism's roots, but it is not associated with one state. Salafism is a school of thought that rejects most innovation and non-Islamic influence but has multiple branches. Many Salfists are apolitical, while others want to be engaged in the political process through legitimate means. Salafi Jihadists, like ISIS, believe in using violent force to implement the reforms they want to create. These groups became more prominent in the 1990s when Islamist groups began engaging in violent resistance to governments and occupying forces in the Middle East. ISIS and other groups believe in a literal interpretation of Islamic holy teachings and believe in their right to control the behavior of other Muslims through intimidation or punishment.

It is important to note that groups like ISIS take ideology to an extreme; there are many Salafists who do not agree

SHARIA

The Islamic tradition of Sharia is one that generates a great deal of controversy. Often associated with harsh punishments, such as stoning and amputation, it is a complex concept. Sharia refers to the legal interpretation of Islamic teachings, including the Koran, sunnah, qiyas, and ijma. Different schools of legal thought have emerged based on how leading legal scholars have interpreted those four religious sources. Rulings are handed down by courts, which exist today in religious communities and govern some religious cases like divorce. Some modern countries with a Muslim majority also derive their legal framework from Sharia, while individual Muslims often interpret the restrictions on behavior in their own way or through trusted religious leaders. For most, Sharia is compatible with average day-to-day life, although under ISIS it has been used to justify extreme brutality as a form of punishment. The group is literal to the point of horror, using outdated modes of punishment that today are associated with torture for even small infractions. The vast majority of Muslims do not agree with this interpretation, and it should not be seen as a reflection of modern Sharia understandings.

with the group's practices and have engaged in peaceful manifestations of their beliefs. But when seen as an extension of these ideologies, ISIS's practices become more targeted and less random. Salafi extremism, like Wahhabism, rejects non-Sunni Islam and other faiths. ISIS has taken this rejection to a new level, forcing conversion to Islam and taking women who are not Muslim as slaves, particularly Yazidi. The group uses teachings from both schools of thought to justify their violent oppression of non-Muslims. This complete rejection of outside influence and literalistic readings of religious texts also help understand why the group carries out their widespread destruction of cultural sites; they are mimicking ancient stories and cleansing their territory.

CULTURAL CLEANSING

In the ancient world, a destruction of structures was a show of strength and domination. Cities were routinely razed to demonstrate the power of a conquering force. Religion was also spread in this way; encroaching forces destroyed religious shrines or icons as a means to force the conversion of populations. But these practices fell from favor when the international

An Iraqi soldier investigates the inside of the destroyed museum in Mosul, Iraq, after the site was recaptured from ISIS in March 2017, on the way to freeing the city.

SAUDI ARABIA

Saudi Arabia is a wealthy gulf state located on the Arab Peninsula. Ruled by the House of Saud, the country is a common source of controversy due to its strict restriction on citizens' behavior, including banning women from driving and other common practices. The country retained a level of independence that other countries in the region did not, staying outside of the Ottoman Empire and never becoming a British or French controlled country. The state is associated with Wahhabism, which is often seen as an extremist strain of Sunni Islam. Saudi Arabia is also associated with extremist groups like al-Qaeda, and it has been accused of supporting groups that ascribe to their particular brand of purist Islamist ideology. Destruction of cultural sites in the country has caused controversy, and it bears resemblances to the cultural erasure with which ISIS engages. But Saudi Arabia does not support ISIS, and it has been involved in efforts to defeat the organization. Even so, the country's fundamentalist bend raises questions about the role of states in protecting their own heritage sites and how ideology can pose a threat to cultural sites even in stable countries.

community began valuing heritage sites as artwork and laws were passed that protected these areas. The changing norms in how we see these spaces has created an environment in which destruction of heritage sites, including religious shrines and temples, is extremely taboo.

But there are numerous examples of Salafist and Wahhabist groups destroying heritage sites in modernity. In the early twentieth century, Saudi Arabia destroyed temples and sites that showed the religious diversity of the country, including the al-Baqi cemetery and signs of Ottoman, pagan, and other influences. In the early 2000s, al-Qaeda began attacking sites in areas where they were active, including the 1,700 year old Bamiyan Buddhas in Afghanistan, the Shia al-Askari mosque in Iraq, and the ancient city of Timbuktu.

ISIS's destruction, then, is not necessarily new. But the rate at which they have been able to destroy ancient sites and shrines has been dizzying and overwhelming, in part because they control an area with a high concentration of these heritage sites. They have also had control of them for a prolonged period; unlike al-Qaeda, the group wants to set up a state of their own, and although they have lost territory in ongoing fighting with various forces against them, the group has held places for multiple years. The fact that people no longer worship at the sites they are destroying and that most of the nonreligious structures are not in use has not deterred ISIS from destroying them; for ISIS, anything that harkens to a non-Islamic way of life must be destroyed. The group has a special department, known as the Committee for the Promotion of Virtue and the Prevention of Vice as it is in countries like Saudi Arabia, devoted to overseeing both the destruction of these sites and other ways of exploiting the rich heritage of the region.

"It makes sense that this is something ISIS does not like if you compare this crossroads of civilizations to the monochromatic views of ISIS, which is extremely simplistic ideology," Yale professor Eckart Frahm told *The Politic* after Palmyra, Syria, was targeted by ISIS.[1]

ISIS themselves have spoken about why they destroy these buildings, writing in their propaganda magazine *Dabiq* that it is as a means to cultivate loyalty to ISIS rather than Syria or Iraq. By erasing the history of these populations, the group hopes to replace the sense of identity many draw from their shared national heritage with an identity tied only to ISIS. One of the goals of ISIS is to unite the former Islamic Empire under religious rule, and the group rejects modern borders and nationalism. For them, statues and temples that are linked to pre-Islamic history are a reminder of a heritage they hope to obscure to the point of nonexistance.

But destruction is also a manifestation of the group's extreme violence. Dr. Zainab Bahrani, director of Columbia University's Mapping Mesopotamian Monuments project and

A museum in Mosul, Iraq, was largely destroyed by ISIS. Cultural sites like museums are targeted by ISIS because they show a history that ISIS does not believe in and wishes to erase.

Edith Porada Professor of Ancient Near Eastern Art and Archaeology, told *ArtNews* in 2015 that she sees the targeting of cultural sites as an extension of ISIS's campaign of ethnic cleansing, saying, "This is not just a destruction of cultural heritage, this is an attempt to erase the representation of groups of people. Thousands of years of history—whether Islamic, pre-Islamic, early Christian, or Yazidi—is being wiped out as ISIS attempts to rewrite it in its own vision. This is a genocide."[2]

DESTROYING RELIGIOUS SITES

ISIS has prioritized destroying religious iconography and shrines, including those belonging to faiths protected in Islam. In the early days of Islam and under the Islamic and Ottoman Empires, Christianity and Judaism were both considered *dhimmi*, or protected persons according to Islamic teaching, due to their shared Abrahamic roots. In exchange for a tax, these religious groups and select others were allowed to live under Islamic rule. In practice, it is disputed how closely this system was followed, and massacres of non-Muslim minorities have been reported throughout history. ISIS claims to follow this system, but in practice they have either forced everyone in their territory to convert or they have carried out widespread persecution, including mass executions.

Such persecution extends to destroying religious sites. This includes ancient religious figures, such as statues of Greek and Roman gods and goddesses, and to buildings and structures

A man walks past a mosque in Mosul that was destroyed by fighting between Iraqi forces and ISIS during an effort to free Mosul from ISIS control in 2017.

associated with modern faiths. In Iraq, ISIS destroyed the St. Elijah's Monastery in 2014, a 1,400 year old structure that had sustained significant damage during fighting between insurgents and US troops in 2003. But Muslim structures are not safe, either; Shia and Sufi tombs and shrines have been targeted by the group, which believes only in Sunni Islam as a true expression of the faith.

DESTRUCTION AS PROPAGANDA

Extremist groups have long used propaganda to spread their message to the world, but ISIS has taken the use of propaganda to another level. The group has proven adept at using social media to bypass mass media outlets, releasing videos and images online for their network of followers and to threaten the West. Their destruction of heritage sites has become a key part of that propaganda machine, one that sends a message to the West that ISIS is making permanent changes to the territory they hold.

But destruction is only one way in which ISIS undermines heritage sites. The group has also made reselling looted goods one of their primary income streams. Antiquities are a significant trade on the black market, and ISIS has sold items they are able to collect for high prices. Although it is impossible to know for sure how much money the group has made on the sale of looted antiquities, it is believed to be in the millions or possibly billions of dollars. Documents found in ISIS held areas even show that the group has a special agency, called the Diwan al-Rikaz, or literally the Department of Precious Things That Come Out of The Ground, which handles both antiquities sales and oil sales.

Because of the secretive nature of ISIS, videos and images they release are often the only way experts can tell what damage has been done until the territory is retaken. ISIS seeks to create outrage with their videos of destruction, showing their ability to act without immediate consequences. This can also help with recruiting, showing the group as powerful and active behind the front lines as they remake their territory into their image.

3

DESTRUCTION IN IRAQ

ISIS shocked the world in 2013 and 2014 when it took control of large parts of Iraq, including the cities of Mosul and Fallujah. It was also in Iraq that the group started making high profile attacks on cultural heritage, releasing photos and videos showing their destruction of artifacts, shrines, and large scale structures in territory they held. The group targeted ancient sites dating to as early as the eighth century BCE, including Khorsabad, Nineveh, and Nimrud. Although some sites, like those in Nineveh, were guarded to ensure looting did not take place, ISIS was able to overtake them easily and used violence to intimidate the guards into abandoning their posts. Iraq's Ministry of Antiquities made a statement in March 2015, saying:

> The hand of terrorism insists upon erasing the history of humanity by erasing the heritage of the land of the two rivers amid the shock and astonishment of the world. We have warned previously and warn now that these gangs with their sick, takfiri ideology will continue to destroy

A member of an Iraqi Christian militia prays beneath the altar of a church in Qaraqosh, Iraq, a predominantly Christian city. Although freed from ISIS in October 2016, the city remains deserted, many of its churches destroyed by the terrorists.

> and steal artefacts as long as there is no strong deterrent, and we still await a strong international stand to stop the crimes of [ISIS] that are targeting the memory of humanity.[1]

It has been in Iraq that the world has seen ISIS's "year zero" approach to remaking the world. In their territory, ISIS

has worked to eradicate anything that existed before the establishment of Islam or anything that does not reflect their own interpretation of Islam. This means destroying religious shrines and temples, including Christian and Shia sites, and burning books they do not believe are Islamic enough.

Iraq, which has suffered wars and looting in the past, has an advantage over war torn Syria. As forces have reclaimed territory from ISIS, experts have been able to move quickly to analyze the damage and safeguard what has been left. The country also has extensive and functional departments dedicated to preserving heritage and stopping the sale of looted goods, which has proven difficult to do effectively. In many cases, artifacts had been taken out of Iraq and placed in other museums prior to ISIS's rise, as seen with the Mosul Museum, which housed replicas of items currently stored safely in Baghdad.

NIMRUD

The city of Nimrud, or Kalhu as it was known at its founding, was built in the thirteenth century BCE, and served as a second capital for the Assyrian Empire. Archaeologists began excavating the area in 1945 and have since found numerous structures, tombs, and artifacts dating back to Assyrian rule. Many of the transportable artifacts, including sculptures and reliefs, were

An Iraqi soldier guards the ruins at the historical site of Nimrud, which was damaged by ISIS. Founded in the thirteenth century, Nimrud is an important cultural site in Iraq and is now being heavily guarded to protect against ISIS retaking the site.

taken to museums in London and New York, which has spared some of the great works found there from destruction by ISIS.

Gates, walls, and former palace ruins have all been found at Nimrud, with inscriptions and artwork heralding the strength of the Assyrian Empire. A wall believed to be the city's demarcation surrounds on area of around 890 acres. Sculptures of kings, including Ashurnasirpal I and II, were found, along with panels

that depict Shalmaneser III's military campaigns between 859–824 BCE. Temples to gods like Nabu and Ishtar were found alongside ziggurats and tombs. These inscriptions and structures provided priceless understanding of life in the region and under Assyrian rule. Most famously, the city is known for *lamassu*, statues weighing tons that depict bearded men with the bodies of lions or bulls and wings. Today, the famous gates at which these sculptures stood have been recreated in museums with *lamassu* that were removed from Nimrud, including an exhibit at the Metropolitan Museum of Art in New York City.

In May, 2015, ISIS moved into Nimrud with bulldozers to begin destroying the archaeological site. Although the extent of the damage they did was unknown until Iraqi forces retook the area from ISIS, the group posted videos and photos of their actions online as part of their propaganda efforts. A rapid response team sent by UNESCO in December 2016, found that ISIS destroyed reliefs and structures around the site using bulldozers and explosives. Among the structures destroyed was the ancient ziggurat, a temple complex that has been one of Nimrud's most iconic structures. It was also found that as ISIS retreated from Iraqi forces, they carried out large scale ad hoc destruction of ancient sites at Nimrud. A local man named Hassan Mahmoud told BBC Radio 4 in 2016:

> The ruins have vanished. History that went back thousands of years was finished off in one night. Fifty years of effort to protect these ruins went in vain. It's a disaster. Our parents and grandparents used to take care of this site. But ISIS destroyed it in one night.[2]

THE GULF WAR

Today, Iraqi sites are in great danger of being looted, either by ISIS or in the aftermath of conflict between ISIS and Iraqi forces. But this is not a new problem for Iraq. Dating to at least the Gulf War of 1990 and 1991, the country has struggled to recover and protect ancient artifacts that were smuggled onto the black market. The Gulf War was a US-led invasion of Iraq that took place after Saddam Hussein, leader of Iraq, invaded and annexed the Gulf state of Kuwait. In the chaos that followed and subsequent uprisings, looting was common in museums and ancient sites, with thousands of artifacts going missing. In the United States invasion in 2003, damage to the Iraq National Museum led to the looting of more precious goods. Some of the items, like Sumerian vases and Akkadian statues, date to 5000 BCE.. Following that period of looting, the country and international community worked to ensure the safety of the museum, closing it until 2015. Today, concerns that looting could again leave the country's artifacts up for sale has prompted a groundswell of funding and programs designed to secure the artifacts now in museums and to stop looting from taking place at cultural sites once held by ISIS.

The team, which included UNESCO officials and local experts, moved quickly to guard what was left at Nimrud and to establish what could be saved. Concerns about looting have risen as ISIS has destabilized once protected areas, and safeguards were put in place to ensure potential black market dealers were not able to steal from the site. What's more, it is believed that most of the artifacts at Nimrud remain underground, and that much of the city itself has not been found. As a result, there is a chance that the site at Nimrud could in time prove to be even larger—and protected from ISIS—than initially believed.

MUSEUMS OF MOSUL & NINEVEH

Mosul is a major city in northern Iraq, located around 250 miles north of the capital Baghdad. Part of the modern city is built on the ruins of the Assyrian capital of Nineveh, which is believed to have once been the largest city in the entire world around its peak in 700 BCE. Along with Mosul, which was historically close to but separate from Nineveh, the two sites have provided remarkable sculptures, artworks, reliefs, tombs, and structures dating to the later centuries BCE.

Mosul played an important role in establishing ISIS as a powerful force in the region. The capturing of Mosul in early 2014 heralded the beginning of their early wave of conquest and destruction, and it was from Mosul that Abu Bakr al-Baghdadi proclaimed the establishment of his supposed caliphate. It has also been the scene of some of the group's most significant cultural destruction, including the ransacking of museums and libraries. In some ways, it was at Mosul and Nineveh that it became clear that ISIS was going to prioritize destroying historical artifacts, a pattern they have since replicated elsewhere in their territory.

An Iraqi soldier fires on ISIS militants outside the museum in Mosul during the March 2017 battle to retake the city from the Islamic State. The museum, along with much of the city, was left in ruins by ISIS.

BAGHDAD

Baghdad is the capital and largest city in Iraq, and it seemed a possible target for ISIS early on in the group's rise. Under al-Baghdadi, the group carried out numerous attacks in the city, and their forces came within a few hundred miles of city limits as they pushed into Iraqi territory from Fallujah and Mosul. In addition to the catastrophic impact ISIS's capture of the capital would have on the country, the city's ancient history would be at risk. Baghdad, a pre-Islamic name for the city, sits in an area where humans have lived for thousands of years. The city itself was built by the Abbasids in 762. Mansur, the caliph of the Islamic Empire, made the city his capital, marking the beginning of a complex and important history. Built to model Mansur's idea of paradise as read in the Koran, the city is an architectural wonder with gardens, homes, and businesses laid out in a round urban design. The city served as a global center of learning from the eighth to the thirteenth centuries, leading to amazing advances in science, literature, mathematics, and other areas of study. After the fall of the Ottomans, it was named the capital of the newly created country of Iraq, and it has since played an important role in Arab and regional politics. Home to numerous mosques, houses of worship, libraries, and cultural sites, it has long been a center of culture in the region, and it is now home to museums that house artifacts that were found at areas now ravaged by ISIS.

In Mosul, ISIS targeted libraries and museums, destroying artifacts and burning thousands of books. The Mosul Museum is Iraq's second largest, and it was home to many priceless statues and artifacts from antiquity. In a video released in February, 2015, ISIS militants can be seen ransacking the museum, taking sledgehammers to statues, and toppling others over. Those that were too big to destroy completely were defaced, including massive winged *lamassu* statues that once stood at the gates of Assyrian palaces. But this wasn't the first time the Mosul Museum was targeted; after the Gulf War in 1990 looting became an issue at the museum, and it is believed that some of the artifacts smashed by ISIS were reproductions rather than originals, many of which are housed in Baghdad.

The group also targeted the University of Mosul library, home to thousands of rare books, many of which were registered with UNESCO. The same month militants ransacked the Mosul Museum, they publicly burned around eight thousand books before setting the building itself on fire. UNESCO called it "one of the most devastating acts of destruction of library collections in human history," with a total of over one hundred thousand manuscripts and books lost.

In Nineveh, ISIS destroyed both the Mosque of the Prophet of Yunus and the Mosque of the Prophet Jerjis. Like Imam Dur Mausoleum, located near Samarra, they demolished these structures completely. The group also destroyed the Mashki and Adad Gates, two ancient structures that had been rebuilt in the twentieth century. ISIS released pictures of both gates showing their complete destruction. According to Michael Danti, codirector of the Cultural Heritage Initiative at the American Schools of Oriental Research and a professor of archaeology at Boston University, ISIS's total erasure of the sites is intended to send a message to those fighting them that the group will leave nothing behind.

الايمان
المتنبي

People in Baghdad, Iraq, buy books to donate to the University of Mosul library. Much of the library's original collection of books and documents was destroyed when the city was taken by ISIS.

"ISIS is essentially sending a signal to the government of Iraq that if they continue with their offensive on Mosul they can expect a scorched earth policy," he told *National Geographic* in 2016.[3]

HATRA

Hatra is an ancient city found between Mosul and Baghdad, and its origins are difficult to determine. As an important trading center, the cities complex ruins include elements of Eastern and Western style and architecture. Held by the Parthians and attacked frequently by the Romans in the early years CE, it has long been one the best preserved Parthian cities in the region. It was home to sculptures, colonnades, gates, streets, and temples to numerous gods, and was named a UNESCO World Heritage Site in 1985.

Harta fell under ISIS control around the time of Mosul and according to reports was used as a training camp. The group released video in spring of 2015 showing militants using sledgehammers, picks, and guns to destroy sculptures, walls,

Hatra, an ancient city in Iraq, is known for its exquisite ruins. Unfortunately, the city suffered serious destruction when it was captured by ISIS jihadists.

and engravings. As in other videos, the group called the statues "signs of polytheism." The militants also directly addressed UNESCO claims that they were committing war crimes by destroying artifacts, saying, "Some of the infidel organizations say the destruction of these alleged artifacts is a war crime. We will destroy your artifacts and idols anywhere and Islamic State will rule your lands."[4] Photos and witnesses later said that explosives and bulldozers were used on larger structures.

Hatra was retaken by Iraqi forces in late April 2017, offering the first chance to see just how much damage the group was able to cause. At time of writing, investigations were still underway. When news broke of the group's destruction of Hatra, UNESCO Director Bokova said, "There is absolutely no political or religious justification for the destruction of humanity's cultural heritage."[5]

Although today we condemn the destruction of artifacts, ISIS does cite religious scripture in their attack on heritage. The group has cited Abraham and Muhammad, both of whom destroyed religious icons in territories they conquered as a means to force conversion of the local populations. ISIS has worked to emulate—in a twisted and warped fashion—a literal interpretation of warfare from the earliest days of Islam; that's why they use methods of torture that were common at that time. Destroying artifacts is another literal means by which they are able to act out their grotesque interpretation of what "pure Islam" should mean and the way a "pure caliphate" should look.

4

DESTRUCTION IN SYRIA

Throughout history, Syria has been an important territory that played a significant role in global trade. Diverse and wealthy, numerous empires made Syrian holdings key parts of their administration, and kingdoms rose and fell in the area. This left behind a fascinating and complex historical record, with ruins influenced by numerous cultures and administration notes that detail the ways in which governments from around the world and in the region functioned. The country has six World Heritage Sites registered with UNESCO, and an additional twelve on a tentative list of possible nominations in the future.

But since the civil war started in 2011, Syria's heritage sites have all been under attack and threat. Bombings and fighting have ravaged urban heritage sites in cities like Aleppo, while looting by the numerous armed groups that are active there have left ancient archaeological sites in near destruction. It is into that chaotic picture that ISIS fits, seizing territory and furthering the rate at which ancient sites are pillaged and ruined. The group has turned looting into a streamlined business, moving at a

Russian soldiers and their working dog clear mines at the ancient city of Palmyra, Syria. Like many other historical sites across the Middle East, Palmyra was targeted for destruction by the Islamic State.

near industrial rate as they sap areas of any potentially valuable goods that can be sold on the black market. At the same time, they have used Syrian territory to create propaganda as they have in Iraq, showing videos of their brutal actions. With no sense of stability as there can be in Iraq, Syria's sites have been caught up in a back-and-forth battle between numerous fighting groups, and ISIS has shown a willingness to move quickly to

destroy areas that might fall from their control.

PALMYRA

Located north-east of the Syrian capital of Damascus, Palmyra is one of the greatest archaeological sites in the world. The city itself was founded as an oasis along a caravan route, and references to the city date back to around 2000 BCE. The city rose in importance when it became part of the Roman Empire in the first century CE. At that time, it was a central link between trade routes connecting the West with China, India, and modern day Iran. In the *New York Review of Books*, Hugh Eakin wrote in 2016, "Connecting Rome and the civilizations of the Mediterranean with Mesopotamia and the empires of the East, Palmyra had been one of the great trading centers of antiquity; for centuries, its incomparable ruins had stood as monuments to Arab glory and Levantine cosmopolitanism."[1] The city was immensely wealthy and influential until around 273 CE, when it sustained considerable damage. The city was discovered and celebrated by travelers in the seventeenth and eighteenth centuries, and after the few inhabitants who still lived in the city were moved in 1932 the site was open to archaeologists.

A helicopter flies over the ancient city of Palmyra, Syria. The city was first documented in the second millennium BCE, and the structures there survived thousands of years before being demolished by ISIS militants.

The city of Palmyra features incredible structures, including colonnades, temples, urban dwellings, and an amphitheater. Its role as a hub of trade made it a melting pot of architectural and artistic styles, and the ruins reflect its Greco-Roman, Arab, Mesopotamian, and Persian history. UNESCO made the city a World Heritage Site in 1980, noting:

> The grand monumental colonnaded street, open in the centre with covered side passages, and subsidiary

cross streets of similar design together with the major public buildings, form an outstanding illustration of architecture and urban layout at the peak of Rome's expansion in and engagement with the East. The great temple of Ba'al is considered one of the most important religious buildings of the 1st century CE in the East and of unique design. The carved sculptural treatment of the monumental archway through which the city is approached from the great temple is an outstanding example of Palmyrene art. The large scale funerary monuments outside the city walls in the area known as the Valley of the Tombs display distinctive decoration and construction methods.[2]

ISIS took control of Palmyra in May 2015, and the international community became immediately concerned that the group might destroy the city. Those fears were validated quickly, as the group began releasing videos and photos that showed the destruction of shrines and statues, decrying the structures as "manifestations of polytheism."[3]

ISIS is aware of what they are doing in places like Palmyra. In 2015, an ISIS commander said on a radio show in Syria, "Concerning the historical city, we will preserve it and it will not

BASHAR AL-ASSAD

Bashar al-Assad is the president of Syria and has been since taking office after the death of his father in 2000. Prior to that he studied ophthalmology in London, but was recalled to Syria when his older brother and the presumed heir to the Assad dynasty passed away unexpectedly. His father seized power in a coup in 1971 and ruled the country with an iron fist until his death. Although Bashar al-Assad ran in an election to follow his father, the election was uncontested, meaning that he was the only candidate on the ballot. Early on, Assad seemed to advocate for reform, and professionals like archaeologists returned to Syria in search of opportunity. But quickly he began crackdowns on dissidents, and inequality continued to plague the country. In 2011, the Syrian Civil War broke out under Assad's regime, and today his legacy is inarguably one of violence and war. His government has been unable to secure heritage sites amidst the fighting, which has largely left the country's cities in ruin. Whether Assad will remain in power is also unclear, as is what his government could do to ensure the safety of cultural sites in a postwar Syria.

be damaged. But what we will do is to pulverize statues that the miscreants used to pray to."[4]

In fact, the group has shown no such restraint. One of the sites they destroyed was the Temple of Baalshamin, a pre-Islamic shrine to the ancient god Ba'al that was built in the first century CE. Well preserved until 2015, ISIS used explosives to damage the interior, which led to the collapse of the outer columns.

In a statement following the destruction of Baalshamin in 2015, UNESCO Director Bokova said:

> The art and architecture of Palmyra, standing at the crossroads of several civilizations, is a symbol of the complexity and wealth of the Syrian identity and history. Extremists seek to destroy this diversity and richness, and I call on the international community to stand united against this persistent cultural cleansing. Daesh is killing people and destroying sites, but cannot silence history and will ultimately fail to erase this great culture from the memory of the world. Despite the obstacles and fanaticism, human creativity will prevail, buildings and sites will be rehabilitated, and some will be rebuilt.[5]

In August 2015, Palmyra became the scene of one of ISIS's most high-profile individual killings. The group murdered Khaled al-Asaad, a historian and scholar who served as the Director of Antiquities of Palmyra for forty years. Following his retirement in 2003, he worked for the Antiquities and Museums Department of the Syrian government, serving as an expert on Palmyra. An award-winning scholar and considered one of the leading Syrian figures in archaeology, Asaad wrote books about Palmyra and translated Aramaic texts, as well as worked with UNESCO and other international organizations to study and advocate for Palmyra.

It is believed that shortly after taking control of Palmyra, ISIS militants began holding Asaad captive. According to reports, they demanded that he tell them where valuable artifacts were hidden and where they could find rumored treasure, including gold. But Asaad refused to give them information,

After Palmyra, Syria, was retaken from ISIS in 2016, it once again became a popular tourist attraction. Here, people pose for a selfie on the site before the start of a concert.

and in retaliation they murdered him in a public execution and decried his cooperation with the international community. It was not the group's only act of violence at the ancient sites; they used the Roman theater in the city as a stage for public executions. After retaking the city from Syrian forces in late 2016, they destroyed the theater that had been left standing using explosives.

Just as the destruction of heritage sites robs the global community of a chance to deepen our understanding of history, so the death of Asaad marked a bloody attack on knowledge. With his death, the Syrian and international communities lost one of their preeminent scholars of ancient history. Although his work remains as a testament to his dedicated to Palmyra and will inform scholars for generations to come, his work was cut short by ISIS's drive to erase history and recreate the world in their own image.

APAMEA

Apamea is an ancient city that falls outside of ISIS's larger area of control. Rather than being in northeastern Syria, where ISIS's territory is centralized, the city is closer to the eastern coast. In the early 300s BCE the city fell under Macedonian rule, and Apamea was fortified and turned into a powerful center of trade. It was used as a military base, as well. In 64 BCE, Pompey brought it under the Roman Empire and it enjoyed a period of growth, with some of the

The ruined remains of the Temple of Bacchus stand in Apamea, Syria. Although Apamea hasn't seen the same kind of destruction other sites have at the hands of ISIS, it has been victim to looting. Looting is a way for ISIS to make money off of their destruction and fund future terror operations.

city's most impressive structures being built. Then, in 115 CE, an earthquake leveled much of the city, which was later rebuilt. Apamea was eventually burned by Persians in 573, invaded by Crusaders in 1106, and once again hit by an earthquake in 1157.

Despite this brief period of influence, Apamea is home to breathtaking ruins, including the Great Colonnade, which stretches for over a mile with columns on either side. Other ruins of the city include a Roman theater and baths, as well as a temple dedicated to Zeus Belos. Residences have been excavated, along with a castle dating to the Crusades and churches built in the sixth century. The Great Hunting Mosaic, one of the site's greatest discoveries dating from the early 400s CE, was removed from Apamea and currently sits in the Cinquantenaire Museum in Brussels.

Apamea has not seen the same kind of destruction that sites like Palmyra have. Instead, it has been overwhelmed by looting, both by ISIS and other groups active in the area. Side-by-side aerial shots show how destructive looting can be. The Great Colonnade, once standing in largely open fields, is now surrounded on all sides by holes and pockmarks left behind by those who have looted from the site. It is impossible to know what looters were able to steal from the site, but the holes—some of which are significant in size and depth—could destabilize the ruins. A Syrian archaeologist summarized it when he told *The New Yorker*, "They just break the places open."[6]

DURA-EUROPOS

Located near the Iraq-Syria border, Dura-Europos is an ancient city that dates to around 300 BCE. It was conquered in waves like much of the area, first by the Parthians, then the Romans, and eventually the Sassanians in a siege between 256–257 CE. Like other Syrian cities, it was a meeting point of cultures, with

ALEPPO

The fight against ISIS is just one facet of an ongoing and complex battle taking place in Syria, and there are numerous heritage sites that are not under ISIS control but remain at risk of destruction. One of them is Aleppo, the country's largest city prior to the beginning of the civil war in 2011 and estimated to be the second largest today. Dating to around 5000 BCE, Aleppo is one of the oldest inhabited cities in the world, with a storied history as the westernmost end of the Silk Road. The city is home to numerous cultural sites, including ancient Roman, Byzantine, Ottoman, and other structures. The Old City, full of narrow roads and *souqs*, is a UNESCO World Heritage Site, with the Citadel of Aleppo noted for its unique architecture. But fighting between rebels and government forces have largely destroyed Aleppo, particularly the outer edges of the city. An estimated 30 percent of the old city has been reduced to rubble, with holes in archways and other signs of ongoing fighting. Once busy centers of commerce have been left deserted, an apt symbol of the impact of cultural destruction across the country.

numerous styles, religions, and innovations that contributed to making it a great hub of commerce. Once an important Roman stronghold—the empire's easternmost in the area—the Sassanians forced the entire population of the city to leave after they took control of it. Unlike cities like Apamea, which were built over or rebuilt, the ruins of Dura-Euopos were simply covered with mud and sand.

Because the city spent most of the Common Era protected under sand and mud, it is one of the most fascinating archaeological sites in the world. Originally discovered in 1885 and excavated in 1922, the city has provided a wide range of historical artifacts, including military equipment and artwork. The city's structures, like temples and tombs, were all well preserved, as were the frescoes and inscriptions that were found on them. The city's main gate—the Palmyrene Gate—was unearthed and provided new insight into the siege that eventually left the city a ghost town.

There were also several important temples and houses of worship preserved in Dura-Europos. A Jewish synagogue with Aramaic inscriptions was also found, one of the most well preserved synagogues of its era. Paintings from the synagogue

The citadel of Dura-Europos was established in the fourth century BCE. Like other historical sites in Syria and Iraq, ISIS attacked the site and destroyed as much as they could.

are one of the earliest biblical narratives we have found, and it was taken to Damascus for conservation. A Christian church, known as the House Church, was also found. Large frescoes and paintings, as well as parchment scrolls, were found inside. A Roman temple to the god Mithras, known as the Mithraeum, has provided greater insight into the deity's following. The city's cultural and religious diversity is one of the most fascinating parts of its heritage. A 2011 *New York Times* article notes that at one temple, "The inscription is in Greek, and a man with a Latin name and a Greek-titled office in the Roman army is shown presenting an offering to Iarhibol, a god of the migrants from the old Syrian caravan city of Palmyra."[7]

Looting began at Dura-Europos before ISIS tightened their control on the area, but it has accelerated significantly since 2014. Satellite images show the once preserved site marked by holes created by looters and blast holes from explosions. An estimated 70 percent of the city has been destroyed either by looting or by destruction, according to experts. According to the United Nations, the site has been "devastated" by looting and targeted excavations using heavy machinery, which have resulted in numerous previously unexamined areas being irreparably damaged. Artwork, coins, statues, and other movable objects have been sold on the black market and may never be seen again.

MARI

Mari, located close to the Iraq-Syria border in the east of the country, was a trading hub that was founded around 3000 BCE. The city lost much of its power and influence around 1600 BCE, making it one of the most interesting sites to chronicle ancient Syrian history. Once the capital of a kingdom, the city is home to temples to multiple ancient gods and an ancient palace of about three hundred rooms, where extensive artwork and paintings have been found. Also found among the ruins were around twenty-five thousand clay tablets that document the city's diplomatic relations, economy, and legal system. These tablets greatly contributed to historians' understanding of life during that time and how governance functioned in ancient Mesopotamia.

Like Apamea and Dura-Europos, Mari has been the scene of extensive looting since 2014, with aerial images showing over one thousand holes being dug in the area. The palace and temples are believed to be the primary focus of looters, and at this time it is unclear if further destruction of artifacts or structures is taking place.

5

THE DESTRUCTION OF CITIES

Destroying ancient sites and looting artifacts isn't the only way ISIS is undermining the cultural heritage of Iraq and Syria. The group has been carrying out a targeted campaign of ethnic cleansing against ethnic and religious minorities in their territories, turning what was once a diverse area into a homogeneous population by force and violence. This kind of abstract reshaping of culture is perhaps ISIS's most dangerous. It ensures that when ISIS is gone, their legacy will be felt and no less damaging than their immediate ability to destroy ancient artifacts.

HOW ISIS IS CHANGING SYRIA & IRAQ

As discussed in earlier chapters, ISIS is not interested just in ruling territory, but in completely reshaping it in an image they see fit. This means remaking the education system, the legal system, governance, and religious practices. The group is not just reactionary, but taking steps to replace the culture they are destroying with their own vision. ISIS does not see themselves as being inevitably defeated, but rather as a multigenerational fighting force destined to defeat their enemies even if the tide turns against them. In ordder for the group to achieve that, however, they need to create their own state, and to do so means creating a culture that aligns with their perverse world view.

YAZIDI

The Yazidis are a Kurdish religious minority in northern Iraq and have been heavily targeted for persecution by ISIS. The group has been the focus of continued campaigns of ethnic cleansing, including holding thousands of Yazidis hostage on Mount Sinjar and forcing women into sexual slavery. Like the destruction of cultural sites, the persecution of minorities is another way ISIS has tried to enforce a homogeneous and uniform culture on the territory they hold. Yazidis are monotheistic and follow a faith that combines elements of Zoroastrianism, Islam, Judaism, and Christianity. It is not possible to convert to Yazidism, and Yazidis are not allowed to marry outside of their faith; there are only an estimated seven hundred thousand in the world, with most of them in northern Iraq. Throughout history the group has been persecuted as devil worshipers, and today ISIS considers them a non-Islamic influence that must be forced from their territory. To do so, ISIS has captured areas where the Yazidis live and executed all men while enslaving women and taking children to be trained as fighters. Hundreds of thousands of Yazidis have been forced to flee to refugee camps far from what has long been their traditional homeland, and it is unclear when they will be able to return and rebuild their lives.

ISIS has created schools where children are taught from a young age to embrace violent ideology, and take children out of formal education early on to train them for military roles. The group has undermined city's ability to function by killing, targeting, or intimidating professionals, including women who have been forced to leave fields like medicine and education.

They have also worked to create a homogeneous society by forcing minorities to flee or killing them. The mass migration of populations shapes culture for generations, and ISIS has undercut what was a tradition of diversity among ethnic and religious groups across Syria. Forcing populations to flee has also caused immense strain on economic resources, and resettling them in the mostly destroyed cities that ISIS now holds will take years to accomplish. For children, this could mean missing out on years of important education, creating a lost generation of Syrian and northern Iraqi children.

In Syria, ISIS is just one of many groups targeting civilians and contributing to a cycle of violence that has left the country destabilized since 2011. But even so, their wanton destruction of territory and life makes the question of what a postwar Syria looks like all the more murky. The layers of problems that have emerged in Syria make it difficult to know how best to secure heritage sites while providing enough resources to

An Iraqi man walks with his child between demolished buildings in Mosul, Iraq. Although many families fled Mosul when fighting between ISIS and Iraqi forces began, others, having nowhere to go, stayed behind.

those impacted by the fighting and helping to rebuild their lives. Continued fighting also means that the areas where ISIS has been forced out of are difficult to secure or even hold; Palmyra has passed between government and ISIS hands multiple times, wreaking further havoc in the already crumbling city.

In Iraq, the aftermath of ISIS control has become stark. The group has left behind almost uninhabitable cities littered with IEDs and traps. They have employed a "scorched earth" policy, determined to leave nothing behind for government forces. By doing so, they are remaking the fabric of the countries where they are active, forcing future generations to carve out a new space for cities that were once among the most prominent in their respective states.

RAQQA

ISIS's cultural destruction can perhaps best be explained with Raqqa, the Syrian city that the group has made its capital-of-sorts since 2014. Raqqa, located in northern Syria, seems to date back to the Hellenistic period under different names. It was not a powerful city under the Roman Empire, but was made an official trading post between the Byzantines and the Persians in the fifth century CE. It was the scene of considerable fighting in the early Islamic era, eventually becoming a significant cultural capital in the late 700s CE. A brief period of decline began in the late ninth century, but served as a customs post for the Ottoman Empire and eventually became the sixth largest city in modern Syria.

In early 2013, militant groups were able to take control of Raqqa, and in early 2014 ISIS was able to force out all rival groups to take complete authority over the city. The city was declared the caliphate's capital, giving it a unique position in ISIS's strategy. The kind of destruction seen in other cities has taken place due to air strikes and combat; photos from inside

Syrian refugees cross the border back into Syria from Turkey after Kurdish forces helped retake the town of Tal Abyad, Syria, from ISIS in June 2015.

Raqqa show the damage to infrastructure. But ISIS has staked the state they hope to build on Raqqa, and they have made it an experiment in how they can create a functioning country. As a result, the blend of all-out destruction and oppression that ISIS seeks to use to erase culture in their territory can be seen in the city.

Aerial images of Raqqa have shown that the destruction ISIS has carried out is different from that in other areas. According to a report by the American Association for the Advancement of Science (AAAS), "Observed damage at Raqqa is different from the other sites discussed in this report. Little damage is a result of direct military conflict. Only scattered craters, suggestive of aerial bombardment or artillery fire, are present. Rather, when damage is present, it appears to be nearly total and targeted, with specific buildings disappearing while the surrounding buildings remain untouched."[1]

This suggests that ISIS themselves are carrying out these targeted attacks, while other damage is being done by air strikes around the city. This is in keeping with ISIS goals of making Raqqa a functional city; widespread destruction would make stability difficult, although the group is not willing to give up its goal of eradicating historical sites that are not in line with their idea of "pure Islam." Many of the sites that have been destroyed within the city limits are shrines and temples, including a Sufi shrine from the Ottoman period and tombs belonging to ancient leaders. The Old City's wall has also shown signs of damage, including blast holes and openings.

Rather than focusing on physical destruction in Raqqa, ISIS has worked to enact their extreme overhaul of education, religion, and behavior that they envision as the norm in their territory. They have persecuted and forced out all religious and ethnic minorities, or forced them to convert to Islam. The group

SHIA ISLAM

Although we often talk about Islam as one faith, there are multiple branches of Islam with distinct beliefs, much like Christianity. ISIS is a Sunni group that fed on disenfranchisement among Iraqi Sunnis early on in their rise to power, although the majority of Sunnis around the world do not agree with the group's ideology or actions. In fact, the majority of Muslims are Sunni, with some estimates putting the rate at around 85 to 90 percent. The other 10 to 15 percent of Muslims are Shiite, adherents of Shia Islam. Shia evolved out of what was once the central Islamic faith after the death of the prophet Muhammad. They believe that Ali, rather than Abu Bakr, was designated as Muhammad's successor as Caliph of the growing Islamic Empire. The group clashed early on with the Sunni majority, and that tension has remained prevalent among politicians rather than religious factions; Iran is the only Shia majority country in the Middle East and is a theocracy, which frequently clashes with Sunni state Saudi Arabia. ISIS has targeted Shia Muslims alongside Christians and Jews, destroying shrines and tombs held holy by Shias. It is just another reason why the group is not truly representative of Islam, and why many consider their religious justifications to be not only retrograde, but ultimately transparent cover for brutal power grabs.

has reshaped school curricula into a method of training children to become soldiers, and forced women back into the home through restrictions on dress, travel, and employment. ISIS has shuttered universities and turned former houses of worship into headquarters, while restricting access to education for adults and using a network of spies to learn when anyone acts or speaks against the group.

While most of ISIS's cultural destruction is thought of as relating to the past and our understanding of it, the actions they take in places like Raqqa are equally damaging. By effectively destroying a city's cultural capacity through destruction of museums, institutions, and sites, the group is able to ensure that if the city is retaken, their impact will be felt for generations to come. They employ a similar yet very different strategy in other cities, where they lay traps and bombs to further destroy urban spaces when they have left.

DESTROYED BY WAR

Targeted destruction of cities is one of the ways in ISIS has torn apart their territory. But there are also concerns about the impact of war. In some cities, particularly in Iraq, fighting between ISIS and security forces are just the latest combat missions to be carried out inside city limits, contributing to an ongoing cycle of violence that has left urban populations reeling. While ISIS makes it a point to hinder the cities in which they rule, their willingness to fight until the very last ensures that whatever is left is largely in ruins by the time security forces are able to secure the territory.

An Iraqi soldier stands guard while a couple of women walk down a destroyed street in Fallujah, Iraq. Although the city has been retaken from ISIS, only 10 percent of homes are habitable.

Fallujah, Iraq, was one of the first cities ISIS took control of, and it was only retaken by Iraqi forces in mid-2016. The city lies in an area that has been inhabited since Babylonian times, and was for most of history a relatively small town along a trade route. It was home to thousands of Jewish residents for centuries. In the twentieth and twenty-first centuries, the city became the setting of numerous battles between Iraqi forces and US-led forces, and became the center of fighting between insurgents and US occupying forces following the 2003 invasion of Iraq.

Because of the consistent fighting in Fallujah up until 2014, the city had sustained significant damage before falling to ISIS. But what Iraqi forces found when they retook the city in 2016 was shocking. Images show a city in complete ruin, littered with trash and with defaced buildings along main roads. This damage was furthered by combat between Iraqi forces and ISIS fighters as the government retook the city. What's more, ISIS left behind traps that could further destroy the city.

Ramadi, another city that spent a considerable amount of time under ISIS rule, fared even worse. The city was nearly annihilated, with its busy Haji Ziad Square left completely empty. Business centers, residential areas, and infrastructure were all left in pieces. Fighters burned universities and other institutions as they fled the city, including large buildings they used as headquarters and for administrative purposes. Homes were used as barracks, leaving them heavily damaged. The destruction did not stop when ISIS was finally pushed out of the city, either; they were able to continue their violence by leaving behind traps and IEDs as they fled. As AP noted, "the Islamic State group is increasingly using a scorched earth strategy as it loses ground in Iraq. When IS fighters withdraw, they leave an empty prize, blowing up buildings and wiring thousands of others with explosives. The bombs are so costly and time-consuming to defuse that much of recently liberated Iraq is now unlivable."[2]

6

PRESERVING HISTORY

At the May 2015 Egyptian launch of #Unite4Heritage, UNESCO Director Bokova said:

> When violent extremists say humanity is not a single community that shares values, when they say world heritage doesn't exist, when they say pre-Islamic heritage is idolatry, when they say that diversity is dangerous, that tolerance and dialogue are unacceptable—we must respond. We must respond by showing that exchange and dialogue between cultures are driving force of all history. We must show that diversity has always been and remains today strength for all societies. Together, we will put forward a new humanist narrative of shared values, of humanity as a single family. Today, we send a clear and resounding message—we do not accept cultural cleansing and we stand together to do everything we can to stop it.[1]

But finding ways to do that is difficult, particularly when war in Syria and fighting in Iraq makes sustained presence around cultural sites far from easy. Despite the difficulties, however,

UNESCO director general Irina Bokova speaks at the National Museum in Baghdad, Iraq, during a visit in 2015. UNESCO is working to protect as many historical sites from ISIS as possible.

there are groups and individuals working to save the historical sites that ISIS is bent on destroying, as well as find unique ways to preserve the heritage that is under threat. This includes individuals who smuggle artwork from behind ISIS lines, museums finding new technologies that can help replicate the lost artifacts, and international groups that are ensuring citizens feel connected to their history.

SAFEGUARDS FOR DAMAGED SPACES

For sites under ISIS control, one of the most important steps in ensuring the site is saved is providing adequate protection once ISIS is forced out. Combat zones are notoriously dangerous for artifacts, which can be looted or vandalized while no one is paying attention. UNESCO works with the international community and local experts to move into areas where heritage sites have been damaged to assess the destruction and ensure that the area is being guarded.

The international community has rallied to help ensure the safety of heritage sites, with France in particular pledging thirty million Euros to a global fund called the Safeguarding Endangered Cultural Heritage conference. "What we have to do today, and what we have managed to do, is to ensure the future of what is precious to humanity," French President Francois Hollande said in 2016 when the pledge was announced. "It is already late."[2]

In some ways, President Hollande is right. For many of the artifacts and structures that ISIS has destroyed, it is too late. Even the best efforts cannot put back together dust. But that does not mean that ISIS's campaign of erasure has been successful. In fact, it has galvanized and rallied the world behind efforts to ensure that ISIS is held accountable. UNESCO has vocally advocated for the group's prosecution on war crimes

France's then-president Francois Hollande (*center*, *standing*) delivers a speech during a meeting of the US-led coalition to fight ISIS. Hollande warned the Western forces to prepare for Islamic State militants to return to cities after they had been recaptured.

charges, and numerous groups are working to document the devastation for use in future trials. With the 2016 sentencing of Ahmad al-Faqi al-Mahdi on charges related to destruction of heritage sites there is formally a precedent for the International Criminal Court to try these sorts of cases, although it may require some finessing of international law to ensure that all the violations can be taken into consideration.

"The question is not so much what laws are in place; the important question is whether there is political will to enforce the laws and whether there are appropriate resources to catch the perpetrators and collect the evidence needed to [convict] them," Rick St. Hilaire, a lawyer specializing in heritage law told *LiveScience*.[3]

TECHNOLOGY

Technology has greatly impacted the way we understand and learn about historical sites, and when it comes to combating ISIS, it is playing a huge role in making sure we understand what is being done to heritage structures. But it is also making it possible to re-create destroyed structures and artifacts so that they can be shared in some form with audiences around the world.

The ASOR Cultural Heritage Initiatives is a partnership between the US State Department and the American School of Oriental Research, aimed at using technology to document the damage being done in Iraq and Syria. The group uses satellite imagery to assess damage, and it works with experts and local volunteers to gather other evidence. A database has been made with information on thirteen thousand cultural heritage sites across both countries, and that information is used to assess new images and information that comes in to get a clear picture of how much damage ISIS has created.

Three-dimensional imaging is also used to re-create ruined structures digitally, something the Syrian government has also begun collaborating on to track before and after status of sites. This information can be used to create replicas, something that has been done on multiple occasions to raise awareness of the devastation. This included a two-thirds size model of the Arch of Triumph in Palmyra, which was first shown in Trafalgar Square in London.

A larger exhibit was set up in Rome, at the Colosseum, in 2016. Called "Rising from Destruction," it included replicas of

A replica of Palmyra's Arch of Triumph is displayed in London's Trafalgar Square. Restoring and displaying replicas of sites destroyed by ISIS is a show of defiance, a way for the people of the world to tell ISIS they won't allow history to be erased.

lamasso, rooms from palaces that have been destroyed, and parts of temples from Palmyra. There were also pieces of statutes that had been destroyed and recovered from ISIS territory.

Francesco Rutelli, a curator for the exhibit, explained that the message of the exhibit was one of universality, and designed to put the cultural heritage of places like Syria and Iraq into a global framework. She told NPR in 2016 that its message is "to show that all that has been destroyed can be reconstructed." Rutelli—who was once Italy's culture minister—says one country's cultural heritage is important for all humankind "because it is our heritage, not only the Syrian or Iraqi or Afghan or Latin American. It's a universal heritage."[4]

But there are questions about what these kinds of replicas mean in the context of the fight against ISIS, namely whether it's possible to honor them while acknowledging the legacy of death and loss that now accompanies them. These questions also plague planning for postwar restoration, another process ASOR is involved with. Allison Cuneo of ASOR told PBS, "That's part of a wider debate about the changing meaning of these places. Palmyra is no longer simply a tourist site. ISIS child soldiers carried out executions in the amphitheater and left behind a mass grave of civilians. How can clean-up and restoration efforts pay homage to that fact?"

SAVING TREASURES

But it's not just major international groups working to save the cultural heritage of Syria and Iraq; locals are doing their part as well. Archaeologists and experts have reportedly been working behind ISIS lines to do what they can to protect books and art, a dangerous business that could cost them their lives.

One of the leaders of efforts to save and document ISIS's destruction is Amr al-Azm, an archaeologist who runs a network of experts who enter ISIS territory to take pictures and gather evidence of ISIS's actions. His team, which he calls the Monuments Men after a similar group that worked behind German lines in World War II, enters ISIS territory and sends their evidence to him, which is then used to pressure the international community into making changes that could hinder ISIS's ability to generate revenue from looted goods. Their work began in 2012 when he led a group of experts and activists into Maarat, Syria, to save the antiquities housed at a museum there. They used sandbags to cover wall-mounted artwork.

"The idea was to cover them up so that if extremists broke into the museum one day, they would be buried," he told *Mother Jones*.[5]

An Italian restoration expert shows a three-dimensional computer model of a funeral relief from Palmyra, Syria. Restorers hope that using three-dimensional printing will help them restore the artifacts destroyed by ISIS.

INDOSSARE GLI INDUMENTI PROTETTIVI
È OBBLIGATORIO PROTEGGERE LE MANI
È OBBLIGATORIO PROTEGGERE GLI OCCHI
È OBBLIGATORIO PROTEGGERE LE VIE RESPIRATORIE

Al-Azm has worked to encourage the international community to do more to preserve antiquities from ISIS, highlighting the importance of these cultural sites in rebuilding the sense of community that ISIS has worked to destroy. In an open letter to the United Nations, he wrote:

> Syria has a resilient sense of identity based on the concept of a shared citizenship around a common history and supported by a long and rich cultural heritage. Once the fighting stops, the people of Syria will need to reconnect with the symbols that unite them across religious and political lines. The country's ancient past will be key to this—protecting Syria's history is about safeguarding its future too.[6]

International groups have responded, including the Smithsonian's Heritage Task Force, which provides al-Azm's team with cameras, packing equipment, and other items. But their work is extremely dangerous, requiring them to travel across the border of Turkey into ISIS-held territory, where if they are caught they could face execution.

The governments of Syria and Iraq are also working to mitigate the damage. A US State Department and Smithsonian partnership called the Iraq Cultural Heritage Initiative is designed to help stabilize Nimrud, provide conservation training to Iraqi officials, and provide upgrades to the Iraq Museum in Baghdad.

More problematically, the Syrian government has called on the international community to help them secure their heritage sites. In an interview with *National Geographic*, the head of the Antiquities & Museums Maamoun Abdulkarim said, "My hope is to see all of the world together in the battle for Palmyric Normandy. It's a Syrian battle, it's an opposition battle, it is the UK, America Russia."[7]

While his call for support is perhaps well meant, it poses a difficult conundrum for the international community. With Syria's civil war raging, any involvement to secure heritage sites could be interpreted as support for the government, which has been accused of widespread violations of human rights. Air strikes and operations against ISIS have secured some sites and won ground in others, but for the sites to be truly safe it is crucial to end the war entirely—something that has so far proven extremely difficult for all parties involved.

REBUILDING CULTURAL IDENTITY

In addition to finding ways to re-create and document the sites damaged by ISIS, organizations are working to raise awareness about the sites themselves and their significance. ISIS is attacking these sites because they are important reminders of the legacy of prior centuries and a living narrative of how humanity has evolved since the dawn of civilization. Understanding cultural heritage is a way for countries to form a sense of common identity, and heritage sites are a way for the world to connect over a shared sense of purpose and history.

The World Heritage Centre is a UNESCO program aimed at raising awareness about all World Heritage Sites through outreach, volunteer programs, and educational programs. Through it, the group releases books and other materials that can be used in classrooms around the world to engage students with world history and culture. The organization also runs the World Heritage Volunteers Initiative, an annual campaign that sends young adults around the world to help with conservation programs and gain skills they can use in careers focused on preserving World Heritage Sites.

UNESCO's #United4Heritage campaign is a youth-focused participatory program that hosts events and works with local

Syrian musicians play on the damaged Roman amphitheater at the ancient city of Palmyra, Syria, for a press event. Although ISIS has destroyed many historical and cultural sites, the world has responded by doing everything they can to save these sites.

organizations and leaders to encourage people to engage with cultural heritage. In April 2017, the campaign hosted a Wikipedia contest, during which people were asked to improve on Wikipedia postings about famed heritage sites around the

world and in a variety of languages. Programs like this encourage citizens to engage deeply with sites in their own countries and in countries around the world, while learning about the history of the spaces and spreading awareness.

Since 2014, ISIS has threatened and destroyed heritage sites that date back to the dawn of civilization. The group's wanton use of destruction as a tool of cultural reform, violence, and propaganda has made headlines around the world, and drawn attention to these important sites in the Middle East. Far from erasing this history, as ISIS has intended to do, their efforts have only underlined how precious and crucial heritage sites are, and rallied the international community behind efforts to support the conservation of culturally important locations.

In 2015, UNESCO Director Bokova placed the attacks on heritage sites by ISIS in the context of a much larger network of threats against antiquities when she said at a symposium:

> Never in the course of recent history have we known such deliberate, systematic and brutal destruction of cultural diversity and heritage. The attacks against Mesopotamia, which gave us writing, the wheel, the rule of law, are an attempt to obliterate the cradle of civilization and our common humanity. The destruction is clearly part of a global strategy of cultural cleansing [...]

HOW YOU CAN HELP

As we've learned, ISIS's path of cultural destruction has caused significant damage and problems for the international community. While it may seem like these problems are best left to major organizations, there are a lot of ways you can help safeguard these global treasures. Here are just a few ideas!

- Host a fundraising drive with friends and make a donation to one of the organizations helping to preserve these important landmarks.
- Talk to your teacher about doing a special project on a World Heritage Site, like Palmyra, to help spread awareness among your peers and classmates.
- Do your own research to learn more about how important these sites were and how they came to be.
- Visit a local museum to see artifacts up close, and see about speaking with a museum expert to learn more about how the items in your local museum's collection fit into a larger historical context.
- Volunteer with a local conservation or preservation group to help safeguard your own local heritage sites and to learn about the history of your own neighborhood!

> It accentuates the disintegration of societies and spreads like a plague in other countries such as Mali, Libya and Yemen. We must respond to these architects of hate who are hijacking history, and make heard another message: that these are not stones and buildings, but values and identities.[8]

World heritage is about more than just individual countries; it's a bridge that connects us all to the evolution of human civilization. Understanding that is an important part of ensuring we all do our part to protect these important sites—and stand up to groups like ISIS that seek to erase history by destroying the evidence of the past.

CHAPTER NOTES

Chapter 1: The Heart of the Ancient World

1. "Convention (IV) respecting the Laws and Customs of War on Land and its annex: Regulations concerning the Laws and Customs of War on Land," *The Hague*, October 18, 1907, http://www.opbw.org/int_inst/sec_docs/1907HC-TEXT.pdf.
2. "Rome Statute of the International Criminal Court," *ICC*, https://|www.icc-cpi.int/nr/rdonlyres/ea9aeff7-5752-4f84-be94-0a655eb30e16/0/rome_statute_english.pdf
3. "Resolution adopted by the General Assembly on 28 May 2015: 69/281. Saving the cultural heritage of Iraq," *Refworld*, http://www.refworld.org/docid/557abec34.html.
4. "UNESCO Director General condemns destruction of Nimrud in Iraq," *UNESCO*, http://whc.unesco.org/en/news/1244/.

Chapter 2: An Ideology of Destruction

1. Sarah Dillon, "A Doctrine of Destruction: ISIS Attempts to Erase History," *The Politic*, May 19, 2016, http://thepolitic.org/a-doctrine-of-destruction-isis-attempts-to-erase-history/.
2. Hannah Ghorashi, "'This Is a Genocide': Art Historian Zainab Bahrani on ISIS's Destruction of Cultural Heritage," *ArtNews*, November 11, 2015, http://www.artnews.com/2015/11/11/this-is-a-genocide-art-historian-zainab-bahrani-on-isiss-destruction-of-cultural-heritage/.

Chapter 3: Destruction in Iraq

1. Kareem Shaheen, "Isis attacks on ancient sites erasing history of humanity, says Iraq," *The Guardian*, March 9, 2015, https://www.theguardian.com/world/2015/mar/09/iraq-condemns-isis-destruction-ancient-sites.
2. Bethan McKernan, "Isis 'destroys thousands of years of culture almost overnight' as it flees Iraqi army near Mosul," *The Independent*, November 15, 2016, http://www.independent.co.uk/news/world/middle-east/isis-mosul-iraq-army-terrorists-destroy-demolish-nimrud-temples-artefacts-a7418136.html.

3. Kristin Romey, "Exclusive Photos Show Destruction of Nineveh Gates by ISIS," *National Geographic*, April 19, 2016, http://news.nationalgeographic.com/2016/04/160419-Islamic-State-ISIS-ISIL-Nineveh-gates-Iraq-Mosul-destroyed/.
4. Kareem Shaheen, "Isis video confirms destruction at Unesco world heritage site in Hatra," *The Guardian*, April 5, 2015, https://www.theguardian.com/world/2015/apr/05/isis-video-confirms-destruction-at-unesco-world-heritage-site-on-hatra.
5. "Islamic State 'demolishes' ancient Hatra site in Iraq," BBC, March 7, 2015, http://www.bbc.co.uk/news/world-middle-east-31779484.

Chapter 4: Destruction in Syria

1. Hugh Eakin, "Ancient Syrian Sites: A Different Story of Destruction," *The New York Review of Books*, September 29, 2016, http://www.nybooks.com/articles/2016/09/29/ancient-syrian-sites-palmyra-destruction/
2. "Site of Palmyra," *UNESCO*, http://whc.unesco.org/en/list/23/.
3. "Syrian archaeologist 'killed in Palmyra' by IS militants," *BBC*, August 19, 2015, http://www.bbc.co.uk/news/world-middle-east-33984006.
4. Beenish Ahmed, "After ISIS Takes Over Ancient Site, U.N. Resolves To Protect Antiquities From Militants," *ThinkProgress*, May 29, 2015, https://thinkprogress.org/after-isis-takes-over-ancient-site-u-n-resolves-to-protect-antiquities-from-militants-d9adeca3c079.
5. "Director-General Irina Bokova firmly condemns the destruction of Palmyra's ancient temple of Baalshamin, Syria," *UNESCO*, http://en.unesco.org/news/director-general-irina-bokova-firmly-condemns-destruction-palmyra-s-ancient-temple-baalshamin.
6. David Kohn, "ISIS's Looting Campaign," *The New Yorker*, October 14, 2014, http://www.newyorker.com/tech/elements/isis-looting-campaign-iraq-syria.
7. John Noble Wilford, "A Melting Pot at the Intersection of Empires for Five Centuries," *New York Times*, December 19, 2011, http://www.nytimes.com/2011/12/20/science/dura-europos-a-melting-pot-at-the-intersection-of-empires.html.

Chapter 5: The Destruciton of Cities

1. "Ancient History, Modern Destruction: Assessing the Status Of Syria's Tentative World Heritage Sites," *AAAS*, https://www.aaas.org/page/

ancient-history-modern-destruction-assessing-status-syria-s-tentative-world-heritage-sites.
2. Susannah George, et al., "Iraq routed IS from Ramadi at a high cost: A city destroyed," *AP*, May 5, 2016, http://bigstory.ap.org/article/627a3057be2544d68aa75897e299a162/iraq-routed-ramadi-high-cost-city-destroyed.

Chapter 6: Preserving History

1. "Media Advisory - Campaign #Unite4Heritage," *UNESCO*, http://www.unesco.org/fileadmin/MULTIMEDIA/FIELD/Cairo/images/Culture/PR3_ENG.pdf.
2. "France pays £24m into new fund to protect cultural heritage sites," *The Guardian*, December 4, 2016, https://www.theguardian.com/world/2016/dec/04/france-new-fund-cultural-heritage-sites-isis.
3. Owen Jarus, "ISIS May Face War-Crime Charges for Destruction of Historic Sites," *LiveScience*, December 12, 2016, http://www.livescience.com/57173-isis-war-crime-charges-for-heritage-destruction.html.
4. Sylvia Poggioli, "Replicas Of Artifacts Destroyed By ISIS 'Rising From Destruction' In Rome," *NPR*, October 10, 2016, http://www.npr.org/sections/parallels/2016/10/10/497350345/monuments-and-artifacts-destroyed-by-isis-rising-from-destruction-in-rome.
5. Bryan Schatz, "Meet the 'Mon uments Men' Risking Everything to Save Syria's Ancient Treasures from ISIS," *Mother Jones*, March 6, 2015, http://www.motherjones.com/politics/2015/02/how-isis-cashes-illegal-antiquities-trade.
6. Amr al-Azm, "Open Letter Calling on UN to Ban Trade in Syrian Artifacts," *The Syria Campaign*, September 25, 2014, https://diary.thesyriacampaign.org/un-ban-the-trade-in-syrian-antiquities/.
7. Kristin Romey, "Antiquities Chief: Syria Needs Global Help to Save Heritage," *National Geographic*, December 1, 2015, http://news.nationalgeographic.com/2015/12/151201-syria-cultural-heritage-antiquities-isis-palmyra-dgam-assad/.
8. "#Unite4Heritage: United Nations University joins UNESCO campaign to protect heritage in danger," *UNESCO*, http://whc.unesco.org/en/news/1272/.

GLOSSARY

archaeological sites Locations where researchers are currently digging and excavating ruins, artifacts, or other ancient items and structures of interest.

black market An informal network of sellers and buyers who deal in illegal goods.

caliphate An ancient form of government that ruled through Islamic law and was controlled by a caliph, who served as both a religious and political leader.

heritage sites Locations that have been identified as having particular significance in a country's history and in some cases are formally administered and protected by UNESCO.

ideology Beliefs or ideas that dictate a person or group's behavior, goals, and practices.

looting The practice of stealing artifacts from museums, archaeological sites, or other areas to sell on the black market.

Mesopotamia Ancient civilization centered on modern day Iraq; one of the most influential in human history.

norms of war Practices that are accepted as part of warfare and conflict, which constantly change over time.

Ottoman Empire Empire centered in modern Turkey that controlled Syria and Iraq, as well as other parts of the Islamic world, from the late 1200s to the early 1900s.

Persia An ancient kingdom and empire in modern day Iran; sometimes used to refer to the country of Iran.

Pre-Islamic Referring to civilizations prior to the rise of Islam in the seventh century CE.

Rashidun Caliphate The "Rightly Guided" caliphate, made up of the first four leaders to follow the prophet Muhammad.

Salafist A school of Islamic thought that emphasizes a return to the values and practices of early Islam; it is not popular with the majority of Muslims around the world.

Shia A branch of Islam that broke with Sunni teachings over the rightful successor to the prophet Muhammad.

Silk Road A trade route stretching from China to the Mediterranean; one of the most important routes of the ancient world.

Sunni A branch of Islam; the majority of Muslims around the world adhere to this interpretation.

taboo A behavior, idea, or practice that is accepted as being outside the norm or dangerous.

terrorist A person or group that uses violence and fear to achieve political goals.

UNESCO United Nations Educational, Scientific, and Cultural Organization; an umbrella group at the UN that oversees cultural and heritage programs.

United Nations An international organization that governs numerous international laws and treaties.

FURTHER READING

Books

Atwan, Abdel Bari. *Islamic State: The Digital Caliphate*. Berkeley, CA: University of California Press, 2015.

Fawaz, Gerges A. *ISIS: A History*. Princeton, NJ: Princeton University Press, 2016.

Khalaf, Farida. *The Girl Who Beat ISIS: Farida's Story.* London, UK: Square Peg, 2016.

Samer. *The Raqqa Diaries: Escape from Islamic State.* Northampton, MA: Interlink Books, 2017.

Websites

ASOR

http://www.asor-syrianheritage.org/

Consortium working to preserve and document destruction at the hands of ISIS.

Council on Foreign Relations

www.CFR.org

Think-tank focusing on international affairs with backgrounds and other information on ISIS

Human Rights Watch

www.hrw.org

International human rights group with information and reports about the abuses taking place under ISIS.

UNESCO

www.en.unesco.org

International organization working to preserve and promote heritage sites.

INDEX